From the Darkness Cometh the Light

From the Darkness Cometh the Light

Or, Struggles for Freedom

Lucy A. Delaney

MINT EDITIONS

From the Darkness Cometh the Light: Or, Struggles for Freedom was first published in 1891.

This edition published by Mint Editions 2021.

ISBN 9781513223049 | E-ISBN 9781513221540

Published by Mint Editions®

MINT
EDITIONS

minteditionbooks.com

Publishing Director: Jennifer Newens
Design & Production: Rachel Lopez Metzger
Project Manager: Micaela Clark
Typesetting: Westchester Publishing Services

Contents

I

"Soon is the echo and the shadow o'er,
Soon, soon we lie with lid-encumbered eyes
And the great fabrics that we reared before
Crumble to make a dust to hide who dies."

In the year 18—, Mr. and Mrs. John Woods and Mr. and Mrs. Andrew Posey lived as one family in the State of Illinois. Living with Mrs. Posey was a little negro girl, named Polly Crocket, who had made it her home there, in peace and happiness, for five years. On a dismal night in the month of September, Polly, with four other colored persons, were kidnapped, and, after being securely bound and gagged, were put into a skiff and carried across the Mississippi River to the city of St. Louis. Shortly after, these unfortunate negroes were taken up the Missouri River and sold into slavery. Polly was purchased by a farmer, Thomas Botts, with whom she resided for a year, when, overtaken by business reverses, he was obliged to sell all he possessed, including his negroes.

Among those present on the day set apart for the sale was Major Taylor Berry, a wealthy gentleman who had travelled a long distance for the purpose of purchasing a servant girl for his wife. As was the custom, all the negroes were brought out and placed in a line, so that the buyers could examine their good points at leisure. Major Berry was immediately attracted by the bright and alert appearance of Polly, and at once negotiated with the trader, paid the price agreed upon, and started for home to present his wife with this flesh and blood commodity, which money could so easily procure in our vaunted land of freedom.

Mrs. Fanny Berry was highly pleased with Polly's manner and appearance, and concluded to make a seamstress of her. Major Berry had a mulatto servant, who was as handsome as an Apollo, and when he and Polly met each other, day after day, the natural result followed, and in a short time, with the full consent of Major Berry and his wife, were married. Two children were the fruit of this marriage, my sister Nancy and myself, Lucy A. Delaney.

While living in Franklin county, Major Berry became involved in a quarrel with some gentleman, and a duel was resorted to, to settle the difficulty and avenge some fancied insult. The major arranged his affairs and made his will, leaving his negroes to his wife during her life-time and at her death they were to be free; this was his expressed wish.

My father accompanied Major Berry to New Madrid, where the fatal duel was fought, and stayed by him until the end came, received his last sigh, his last words, and closed his dying eyes, and afterwards conveyed the remains of his best friend to the bereaved family with a sad heart. Though sympathizing deeply with them in their affliction, my father was much disturbed as to what disposition would be made of him, and after Major Berry was consigned with loving hands to his last resting place, these haunting thoughts obtruded, even in his sleeping hours.

A few years after, Major Berry's widow married Robert Wash, an eminent lawyer, who afterwards became Judge of the Supreme Court. One child was born to them, who, when she grew to womanhood, became Mrs. Francis W. Goode, whom I shall always hold in grateful remembrance as long as life lasts, and God bless her in her old age, is my fervent prayer for her kindness to me, a poor little slave girl!

We lived in the old "Wash" mansion sometime after the marriage of the Judge, until their daughter Frances was born. How well I remember those happy days! Slavery had no horror then for me, as I played about the place, with the same joyful freedom as the little white children. With mother, father and sister, a pleasant home and surroundings, what happier child than I!

As I carelessly played away the hours, mother's smiles would fade away, and her brow contract into a heavy frown. I wondered much thereat, but the time came—ah! only too soon, when I learned the secret of her ever-changing face!

II

M rs. Wash lost her health, and, on the advice of a physician, went to Pensacola, Florida, accompanied by my mother. There she died, and her body was brought back to St. Louis and there interred. After Mrs. Wash's death, the troubles of my parents and their children may be said to have really commenced.

Though in direct opposition to the will of Major Berry, my father's quondam master and friend, Judge Wash tore my father from his wife and children and sold him "way down South!"

Slavery! cursed slavery! what crimes has it invoked! and, oh! what retribution has a righteous God visited upon these traders in human flesh! The rivers of tears shed by us helpless ones, in captivity, were turned to lakes of blood! How often have we cried in our anguish, "Oh! Lord, how long, how long?" But the handwriting was on the wall, and tardy justice came at last and avenged the woes of an oppressed race! Chickamauga, Shiloh, Atlanta and Gettysburgh, spoke in thunder tones! John Brown's body had indeed marched on, and we, the ransomed ones, glorify God and dedicate ourselves to His service, and acknowledge His greatness and goodness in rescuing us from such bondage as parts husband from wife, the mother from her children, aye, even the babe from her breast!

Major Berry's daughter Mary, shortly after, married H.S. Cox, of Philadelphia, and they went to that city to pass their honeymoon, taking my sister Nancy with them as waiting-maid. When my father was sold South, my mother registered a solemn vow that her children should not continue in slavery all their lives, and she never spared an opportunity to impress it upon us, that we must get our freedom whenever the chance offered. So here was an unlooked-for avenue of escape which presented much that was favorable in carrying out her desire to see Nancy a free woman.

Having been brought up in a free State, mother had learned much to her advantage, which would have been impossible in a slave State, and which she now proposed to turn to account for the benefit of her daughter. So mother instructed my sister not to return with Mr. and Mrs. Cox, but to run away, as soon as chance offered, to Canada, where a friend of our mother's lived who was also a runaway slave, living in freedom and happiness in Toronto.

As the happy couple wandered from city to city, in search of pleasure, my sister was constantly turning over in her mind various plans of escape. Fortune finally favored Nancy, for on their homeward trip they stopped at Niagara Falls for a few days. In her own words I will describe her escape:

"In the morning, Mr. and Mrs. Cox went for a drive, telling me that I could have the day to do as I pleased. The shores of Canada had been tantalizing my longing gaze for some days, and I was bound to reach there long before my mistress returned. So I locked up Mrs. Cox's trunk and put the key under the pillow, where I was sure she would find it, and I made a strike for freedom! A servant in the hotel gave me all necessary information and even assisted me in getting away. Some kind of a festival was going on, and a large crowd was marching from the rink to the river, headed by a band of music. In such a motley throng I was unnoticed, but was trembling with fear of being detected. It seemed an age before the ferry boat arrived, which at last appeared, enveloped in a gigantic wreath of black smoke. Hastily I embarked, and as the boat stole away into the misty twilight and among crushing fields of ice, though the air was chill and gloomy, I felt the warmth of freedom as I neared the Canada shore. I landed, without question, and found my mother's friend with but little difficulty, who assisted me to get work and support myself. Not long afterwards, I married a prosperous farmer, who provided me with a happy home, where I brought my children into the world without the sin of slavery to strive against."

On the return of Mrs. Cox to St. Louis she sent for my mother and told her that Nancy had run away. Mother was very thankful, and in her heart arose a prayer of thanksgiving, but outwardly she pretended to be vexed and angry. Oh! the impenetrable mask of these poor black creatures! how much of joy, of sorrow, of misery and anguish have they hidden from their tormentors!

I was a small girl at that time, but remember how wildly mother showed her joy at Nancy's escape when we were alone together. She would dance, clap her hands, and, waving them above her head, would indulge in one of those weird negro melodies, which so charm and fascinate the listener.

Mrs. Cox commenced housekeeping on a grand and extended scale, having a large acquaintance, she entertained lavishly. My mother cared for the laundry, and I, who was living with a Mrs. Underhill, from New York, and was having rather good times, was compelled to go live with Mrs. Cox to mind the baby. My pathway was thorny enough, and though there may be no roses without thorns, I had thorns in plenty with no roses.

I was beginning to plan for freedom, and was forever on the alert for a chance to escape and join my sister. I was then twelve years old, and often talked the matter over with mother and canvassed the probabilities of both of us getting away. No schemes were too wild for us to consider! Mother was especially restless, because she was a free woman up to the time of her being kidnapped, so the injustice and weight of slavery bore more heavily upon her than upon me. She did not dare to talk it over with anyone for fear that they would sell her further down the river, so I was her only confidant. Mother was always planning and getting ready to go, and while the fire was burning brightly, it but needed a little more provocation to add to the flames.

III

M rs. Cox was always very severe and exacting with my mother, and one occasion, when something did not suit her, she turned on mother like a fury, and declared, "I am just tired out with the 'white airs' you put on, and if you don't behave differently, I will make Mr. Cox sell you down the river at once."

Although mother turned grey with fear, she presented a bold front and retorted that "she didn't care, she was tired of that place, and didn't like to live there, nohow." This so infuriated Mr. Cox that he cried, "How dare a negro say what she liked or what she did not like; and he would show her what he should do."

So, on the day following, he took my mother to an auction-room on Main Street and sold her to the highest bidder, for five hundred and fifty dollars. Oh! God! the pity of it! "In the home of the brave and the land of the free," in the sight of the stars and stripes—that symbol of freedom—sold away from her child, to satisfy the anger of a peevish mistress!

My mother returned to the house to get her few belongings, and straining me to her breast, begged me to be a good girl, that she was going to run away, and would buy me as soon as she could. With all the inborn faith of a child, I believed it most fondly, and when I heard that she had actually made her escape, three weeks after, my heart gave an exultant throb and cried, "God is good!"

A large reward was offered, the bloodhounds (curse them and curse their masters) were set loose on her trail. In the day time she hid in caves and the surrounding woods, and in the night time, guided by the wondrous North Star, that blessed lodestone of a slave people, my mother finally reached Chicago, where she was arrested by the negro-catchers. At this time the Fugitive Slave Law was in full operation, and it was against the law of the whole country to aid and protect an escaped slave; not even a drink of water, for the love of the Master, might be given, and those who dared to do it (and there were many such brave hearts, thank God!) placed their lives in danger.

The presence of bloodhounds and "nigger-catchers" in their midst, created great excitement and scandalized the community. Feeling ran high and hundreds of people gathered together and declared that mother should not be returned to slavery; but fearing that Mr. Cox would wreak his vengeance upon me, my mother finally gave herself up to her captors, and returned to St. Louis. And so the mothers of Israel have been ever slain through their deepest affections!

After my mother's return, she decided to sue for her freedom, and for that purpose employed a good lawyer. She had ample testimony to prove that she was kidnapped, and it was so fully verified that the jury decided that she was a free woman, and papers were made out accordingly.

In the meanwhile, Miss Martha Berry had married Mr. Mitchell and taken me to live with her. I had never been taught to work, as playing with the babies had been my sole occupation; therefore, when Mrs. Mitchell commanded me to do the weekly washing and ironing, I had no more idea how it was to be done than Mrs. Mitchell herself. But I made the effort to do what she required, and my failure would have been amusing had it not been so appalling. In those days filtering was unknown and the many ways of clearing water were to me an unsolved riddle. I never had to do it, so it never concerned me how the clothes were ever washed clean.

As the Mississippi water was even muddier than now, the results of my washing can be better imagined than described. After soaking and boiling the clothes in its earthy depths, for a couple of days, in vain attempt to get them clean, and rinsing through several waters, I found the clothes were getting darker and darker, until they nearly approximated my own color. In my despair, I frantically rushed to my mother and sobbed out my troubles on her kindly breast. So in the morning, before the white people had arisen, a friend of my mother came to the house and washed out the clothes. During all this time, Mrs. Mitchell was scolding vigorously, saying over and over again, "Lucy, you do not want to work, you are a lazy, good-for-nothing nigger!" I was angry at being called a nigger, and replied, "You don't know nothing, yourself, about it, and you expect a poor ignorant girl to know more than you do yourself; if you had any feeling you would get somebody to teach me, and then I'd do well enough."

She then gave me a wrapper to do up, and told me if I ruined that as I did the other clothes, she would whip me severely. I answered, "You have no business to whip me. I don't belong to you."

My mother had so often told me that she was a free woman and that I should not die a slave, I always had a feeling of independence, which would invariably crop out in these encounters with my mistress; and when I thus spoke, saucily, I must confess, she opened her eyes in angry amazement and cried:

"You *do* belong to me, for my papa left you to me in his will, when you were a baby, and you ought to be ashamed of yourself to talk so to one that you have been raised with; now, you take that wrapper, and if you don't do it up properly, I will bring you up with a round turn."

Without further comment, I took the wrapper, which was too handsome to trust to an inexperienced hand, like Mrs. Mitchell very well knew I was, and washed it, with the same direful results as chronicled before. But I could not help it, as heaven is my witness. I was entirely and hopelessly ignorant! But of course my mistress would not believe it, and declared over and over again, that I did it on purpose to provoke her and show my defiance of her wishes. In vain did I disclaim any such intentions. She was bound to carry out her threat of whipping me.

I rebelled against such government, and would not permit her to strike me; she used shovel, tongs and broomstick in vain, as I disarmed her as fast as she picked up each weapon. Infuriated at her failure, my opposition and determination not to be whipped, Mrs. Mitchell declared she would report me to Mr. Mitchell and have him punish me.

When her husband returned home, she immediately entered a list of complaints against me as long as the moral law, including my failure to wash her clothes properly, and her inability to break my head for it; the last indictment seemed to be the heaviest she could bring against me. I was in the shadow of the doorway as the woman raved, while Mr. Mitchell listened patiently until the end of his wife's grievances reached an appeal to him to whip me with the strength that a man alone could possess.

Then he declared, "Martha, this thing of cutting up and slashing servants is something I know nothing about, and positively will not do. I don't believe in slavery, anyhow; it is a curse on this land, and I wish we were well rid of it."

"Mr. Mitchell, I will not have that saucy baggage around this house, for if she finds you won't whip her, there will be no living with her, so you shall just sell her, and I insist upon it."

"Well, Martha," he answered, "I found the girl with you when we were married, and as you claim her as yours, I shall not interpose any objections to the disposal of what you choose to call your property, in any manner you see fit, and I will make arrangements for selling her at once."

I distinctly overheard all that was said, and was just as determined not to be sold as I was not to be whipped. My mother's lawyer had told her to caution me never to go out of the city, if, at anytime, the white people wanted me to go, so I was quite settled as to my course, in case Mr. Mitchell undertook to sell me.

Several days after this conversation took place, Mrs. Mitchell, with her baby and nurse, Lucy Wash, made a visit to her grandmother's, leaving orders that I should be sold before her return; so I was not surprised to be ordered by Mr. Mitchell to pack up my clothes and get ready to go down the river, for I was to be sold that morning, and leave, on the steamboat Alex. Scott, at 3 o'clock in the afternoon.

"Can't I go see my mother, first?" I asked.

"No," he replied, not very gently, "there is no time for that, you can see her when you come back. So hurry up and get ready, and let us have no more words about it!"

How I did hate him! To hear him talk as if I were going to take a pleasure trip, when he knew that if he sold me South, as he intended, I would never see my dear mother again.

However, I hastily ran up stairs and packed my trunk, but my mother's injunction, "never to go out of the city," was ever present in my mind.

Mr. Mitchell was Superintendent of Indian Affairs, his office being in the dwelling house, and I could hear him giving orders to his clerk, as I ran lightly down the stairs, out of the front door to the street, and with fleet foot, I skimmed the road which led to my mother's door, and, reaching it, stood trembling in every limb with terror and fatigue.

I could not gain admittance, as my mother was away to work and the door was locked. A white woman, living next door, and who was always friendly to mother, told me that she would not return until night. I clasped my hands in despair and cried, "Oh! the white people have sold me, and I had to run away to keep from being sent down the river."

This white lady, whose name I am sorry I cannot remember, sympathized with me, as she knew my mother's story and had written many letters for her, so she offered me the key of her house, which, fortunately, fitted my mother's door, and I was soon inside, cowering with fear in the darkness, magnifying every noise and every passing wind, until my imagination had almost converted the little cottage into a boat, and I was steaming down South, away from my mother, as fast as I could go.

Late at night mother returned, and was told all that had happened, and after getting supper, she took me to a friend's house for concealment, until the next day.

As soon as Mr. Mitchell had discovered my unlooked-for departure, he was furious, for he did not think I had sense enough to run away; he accused the coachman of helping me off, and, despite the poor man's denials, hurried him away to the calaboose and put him under the lash, in order to force a confession. Finding this course unavailing, he offered a reward to the negro catchers, on the same evening, but their efforts were equally fruitless.

IV

On the morning of the 8th of September, 1842, my mother sued Mr. D.D. Mitchell for the possession of her child, Lucy Ann Berry. My mother, accompanied by the sheriff, took me from my hiding-place and conveyed me to the jail, which was located on Sixth Street, between Chestnut and Market, where the Laclede Hotel now stands, and there met Mr. Mitchell, with Mr. H.S. Cox, his brother-in-law.

Judge Bryant Mullanphy read the law to Mr. Mitchell, which stated that if Mr. Mitchell took me back to his house, he must give bond and security to the amount of two thousand dollars, and furthermore, I should not be taken out of the State of Missouri until I had a chance to prove my freedom. Mr. H.S. Cox became his security and Mr. Mitchell gave bond accordingly, and then demanded that I should be put in jail.

"Why do you want to put that poor young girl in jail?" demanded my lawyer. "Because," he retorted, "her mother or some of her crew might run her off, just to make me pay the two thousand dollars; and I would like to see her lawyer, or any other man, in jail, that would take up a d—— nigger case like that."

"You need not think, Mr. Mitchell," calmly replied Mr. Murdock, "because my client is colored that she has no rights, and can be cheated out of her freedom. She is just as free as you are, and the Court will so decide it, as you will see."

However, I was put in a cell, under lock and key, and there remained for seventeen long and dreary months, listening to the

> "—foreign echoes from the street,
> Faint sounds of revel, traffic, conflict keen—
> And, thinking that man's reiterated feet
> Have gone such ways since e'er the world has been,
> I wondered how each oft-used tone and glance
> Retains its might and old significance."

My only crime was seeking for that freedom which was my birthright! I heard Mr. Mitchell tell his wife that he did not believe in slavery, yet, through his instrumentality, I was shut away from the sunlight, because he was determined to prove me a slave, and thus keep me in bondage. Consistency, thou art a jewel!

At the time my mother entered suit for her freedom, she was not instructed to mention her two children, Nancy and Lucy, so the white people took advantage of this flaw, and showed a determination to use every means in their power to prove that I was not her child.

This gave my mother an immense amount of trouble, but she had girded up her loins for the fight, and, knowing that she was right, was resolved, by the help of God and a good lawyer, to win my case against all opposition.

After advice by competent persons, mother went to Judge Edward Bates and begged him to plead the case, and, after fully considering the proofs and learning that my mother was a poor woman, he consented to undertake the case and make his charges only sufficient to cover his expenses. It would be well here to give a brief sketch of Judge Bates, as many people wondered that such a distinguished statesman would take up the case of an obscure negro girl.

Edward Bates was born in Belmont, Goochland county, Va., September, 1793. He was of Quaker descent, and inherited all the virtues of that peace-loving people. In 1812, he received a midshipman's warrant, and was only prevented from following the sea by the influence of his mother, to whom he was greatly attached. Edward emigrated to Missouri in 1814, and entered upon the practice of law, and, in 1816, was appointed prosecuting lawyer for the St. Louis Circuit. Toward the close of the same year, he was appointed Attorney General for the new State of Missouri, and in 1826, while yet a young man, was elected representative to congress as an anti-Democrat, and served one term. For the following twenty-five years, he devoted himself to his profession, in which he was a shining light. His probity and uprightness attracted to him a class of people who were in the right and only sought justice, while he repelled, by his virtues, those who traffic in the miseries or mistakes of unfortunate people, for they dared not come to him and seek counsel to aid them in their villainy.

In 1847, Mr. Bates was delegate to the Convention for Internal Improvement, held in Chicago, and by his action he came prominently before the whole country. In 1850, President Fillmore offered him the portfolio of Secretary of War, which he declined. Three years later, he accepted the office of Judge of St. Louis Land Court.

When the question of the repeal of the Missouri Compromise was agitated, he earnestly opposed it, and thus became identified with the "free labor" party in Missouri, and united with it, in opposition to the admission of Kansas under the Lecompton Constitution. He afterwards became a prominent anti-slavery man, and in 1859 was mentioned as a candidate for the presidency. He was warmly supported by his own State, and for a time it seemed that the opposition to Governor Seward might concentrate on him. In the National Republican Convention, 1860, he received forty-eight votes on the first ballot, but when it became apparent that Abraham Lincoln was the favorite, Mr. Bates withdrew his name. Mr. Lincoln appointed Judge Bates Attorney General, and while in the Cabinet he acted a dignified, safe and faithful part. In 1864, he resigned his office and returned to his home in St. Louis, where he died in 1869, surrounded by his weeping family.

"—loved at home, revered abroad.
Princes and lords are but the breath of kings,
'An honest man's the noblest work of God.'"

On the 7th of February, 1844, the suit for my freedom began. A bright, sunny day, a day which the happy and care-free would drink in with a keen sense of enjoyment. But my heart was full of bitterness; I could see only gloom which seemed to deepen and gather closer to me as I neared the courtroom. The jailer's sister-in-law, Mrs. Lacy, spoke to me of submission and patience; but I could not feel anything but rebellion against my lot. I could not see one gleam of brightness in my future, as I was hurried on to hear my fate decided.

Among the most important witnesses were Judge Robert Wash and Mr. Harry Douglas, who had been an overseer on Judge Wash's farm, and also Mr. MacKeon, who bought my mother from H.S. Cox, just previous to her running away.

Judge Wash testified that "the defendant, Lucy A. Berry, was a mere infant when he came in possession of Mrs. Fannie Berry's estate, and that he often saw the child in the care of its reputed mother, Polly, and to his best knowledge and belief, he thought Lucy A. Berry was Polly's own child."

Mr. Douglas and Mr. MacKeon corroborated Judge Wash's statement. After the evidence from both sides was all in, Mr. Mitchell's lawyer, Thomas Hutchinson, commenced to plead. For one hour, he talked so bitterly against me and against my being in possession of my liberty that I was trembling, as if with ague, for I certainly thought everybody must believe him; indeed I almost believed the dreadful things he said, myself, and as I listened I closed my eyes with sickening dread, for I could just see myself floating down the river, and my heart-throbs seemed to be the throbs of the mighty engine which propelled me from my mother and freedom forever!

Oh! what a relief it was to me when he finally finished his harangue and resumed his seat! As I never heard anyone plead before, I was very much alarmed, although I knew in my heart that every word he uttered was a lie! Yet, how was I to make people believe? It seemed a puzzling question!

Judge Bates arose, and his soulful eloquence and earnest pleading made such an impression on my sore heart, I listened with renewed hope. I felt the black storm clouds of doubt and despair were fading away, and that I was drifting into the safe harbor of the realms of truth. I felt as if everybody *must* believe *him*, for he clung to the truth, and I wondered how Mr. Hutchinson could so lie about a poor defenseless girl like me.

Judge Bates chained his hearers with the graphic history of my mother's life, from the time she played on Illinois banks, through her trials in slavery, her separation from her husband, her efforts to become free, her voluntary return to slavery for the sake of her child, Lucy, and her subsequent efforts in securing her own freedom. All these incidents he lingered over step by step, and concluding, he said:

"Gentlemen of the jury, I am a slave-holder myself, but, thanks to the Almighty God, I am above the base principle of holding anybody a slave that has as good right to her freedom as this girl has been proven to have; she was free before she was born; her mother was free, but kidnapped in her youth, and sacrificed to the greed of negro traders, and no free woman can give birth to a slave child, as it is in direct violation of the laws of God and man!"

At this juncture he read the affidavit of Mr. A. Posey, with whom my mother lived at the time of her abduction; also affidavits of Mr. and Mrs. Woods, in corroboration of the previous facts duly set forth. Judge Bates then said:

"Gentlemen of the jury, here I rest this case, as I would not want any better evidence for one of my own children. The testimony of Judge Wash is alone sufficient to substantiate the claim of Polly Crockett Berry to the defendant as being her own child."

The case was then submitted to the jury, about 8 o'clock in the evening, and I was returned to the jail and locked in the cell which I had occupied for seventeen months, filled with the most intense anguish.

V

"There's a joy in every sorrow,
There's a relief from every pain;
Though today 'tis dark tomorrow
HE will turn all bright again."

B efore the sheriff bade me goodnight he told me to be in readiness at nine o'clock on the following morning to accompany him back to court to hear the verdict. My mother was not at the trial. She had lingered many days about the jail expecting my case would be called, and finally when called to trial the dear, faithful heart was not present to sustain me during that dreadful speech of Mr. Hutchinson. All night long I suffered agonies of fright, the suspense was something awful, and could only be comprehended by those who have gone through some similar ordeal.

I had missed the consolation of my mother's presence, and I felt so hopeless and alone! Blessed mother! how she clung and fought for me. No work was too hard for her to undertake. Others would have flinched before the obstacles which confronted her, but undauntedly she pursued her way, until my freedom was established by every right and without a questioning doubt!

On the morning of my return to Court, I was utterly unable to help myself. I was so overcome with fright and emotion,—with the alternating feelings of despair and hope—that I could not stand still long enough to dress myself. I trembled like an aspen leaf; so I sent a message to Mrs. Lacy to request permission for me to go to her room, that she might assist me in dressing. I had done a great deal of sewing for Mrs. Lacy, for she had showed me much kindness, and was a good Christian. She gladly assisted me, and under her willing hands I was soon made ready, and, promptly at nine o'clock, the sheriff called and escorted me to the courthouse.

On our way thither, Judge Bates overtook us. He lived out a short distance in the country, and was riding on horseback. He tipped his hat to me as politely as if I were the finest lady in the land, and cried out, "Good morning Miss Lucy, I suppose you had pleasant dreams last night!" He seemed so bright and smiling that I was imbued with renewed hope; and when he addressed the sheriff with "Good morning Sir. I don't suppose the jury was out twenty minutes were they?" and the sheriff replied "oh! no, sir," my heart gave a leap, for I was sure that my fate was decided for weal or woe.

I watched the judge until he turned the corner and desiring to be relieved of suspense from my pent-up anxiety, I eagerly asked the sheriff if I were free, but he gruffly answered that "he didn't know." I was sure he did know, but was too mean to tell me. How could he have been so flinty, when he must have seen how worried I was.

At last the courthouse was reached and I had taken my seat in such a condition of helpless terror that I could not tell one person from another. Friends and foes were as one, and vainly did I try to distinguish them. My long confinement, burdened with harrowing anxiety, the sleepless night I had just spent, the unaccountable absence of my mother, had brought me to an indescribable condition. I felt dazed, as if I were no longer myself. I seemed to be another person—an on-looker—and in my heart dwelt a pity for the poor, lonely girl, with down-cast face, sitting on the bench apart from anyone else in that noisy room. I found myself wondering where Lucy's mother was, and how she would feel if the trial went against her; I seemed to have lost all feeling about it, but was speculating what Lucy would do, and what her mother would do, if the hand of Fate was raised against poor Lucy! Oh! how sorry I did feel for myself!

At the sound of a gentle voice, I gathered courage to look upward, and caught the kindly gleam of Judge Bates' eyes, as he bent his gaze upon me and smilingly said, "I will have you discharged in a few minutes, Miss Lucy!"

Someother business occupied the attention of the Court, and when I had begun to think they had forgotten all about me, Judge Bates arose and said calmly, "Your Honor, I desire to have this girl, Lucy A. Berry, discharged before going into any other business."

Judge Mullanphy answered "Certainly!" Then the verdict was called for and rendered, and the jurymen resumed their places. Mr. Mitchell's lawyer jumped up and exclaimed:

> "Your Honor, my client demands that this girl be remanded to jail. He does not consider that the case has had a fair trial, I am not informed as to what course he intends to pursue, but I am now expressing his present wishes?"

Judge Bates was on his feet in a second and cried: "For shame! is it not enough that this girl has been deprived of her liberty for a year and a half, that you must still pursue her after a fair and impartial trial before a jury, in which it was clearly proven and decided that she had every right to freedom? I demand that she be set at liberty at once!"

"I agree with Judge Bates," responded Judge Mullanphy, "and the girl may go!"

Oh! the overflowing thankfulness of my grateful heart at that moment, who could picture it? None but the good God above us! I could have kissed the feet of my deliverers, but I was too full to express my thanks, but with a voice trembling with tears I tried to thank Judge Bates for all his kindness.

As soon as possible, I returned to the jail to bid them all goodbye and thank them for their good treatment of me while under their care. They rejoiced with me in my good fortune and wished me much success and happiness in years to come.

I was much concerned at my mother's prolonged absence, and was deeply anxious to meet her and sob out my joy on her faithful bosom. Surely it was the hands of God which prevented mother's presence at the trial, for broken down with anxiety and loss of sleep on my account, the revulsion of feeling would have been greater than her over-wrought heart could have sustained.

As soon as she heard of the result, she hurried to meet me, and hand in hand we gazed into each other's eyes and saw the light of freedom there, and we felt in our hearts that we could with one accord cry out: "Glory to God in the highest, and peace and good will towards men."

Dear, dear mother! how solemnly I invoke your spirit as I review these trying scenes of my girlhood, so long agone! Your patient face and neatly-dressed figure stands ever in the foreground of that checkered time; a figure showing naught to an on-looker but the common place virtues of an honest woman! Never would an ordinary observer connect those virtues with aught of heroism or greatness, but to me they are as bright rays as ever emanated from the lives of the great ones of earth, which are portrayed on historic pages—to me, the qualities of her true, steadfast heart and noble soul become "a constellation, and is tracked in Heaven straightway."

VI

After the trial was over and my mother had at last been awarded the right to own her own child, her next thought reverted to sister Nancy, who had been gone so long, and from whom we had never heard, and the greatest ambition mother now had was to see her child Nancy. So, we earnestly set ourselves to work to reach the desired end, which was to visit Canada and seek the long-lost girl. My mother being a first-class laundress, and myself an expert seamstress, it was easy to procure all the work we could do, and command our own prices. We found, as well as the whites, a great difference between slave and free labor, for while the first was compulsory, and, therefore, at the best, perfunctory, the latter must be superior in order to create a demand, and realizing this fully, mother and I expended the utmost care in our respective callings, and were well rewarded for our efforts.

By exercising rigid economy and much self-denial, we, at last, accumulated sufficient to enable mother to start for Canada, and oh! how rejoiced I was when that dear, overworked mother approached the time, when her hard-earned and long-deferred holiday was about to begin. The uses of adversity is a worn theme, and in it there is much of weak cant, but when it is considered how much of sacrifice the poverty-stricken must bear in order to procure the slightest gratification, should it not impress the thinking mind with amazement, how much of fortitude and patience the honest poor display in the exercise of self-denial! Oh! ye prosperous! prate of the uses of adversity as poetically as you please, we who are obliged to learn of them by bitter experience would greatly prefer a change of surroundings.

Mother arrived in Toronto two weeks after she left St. Louis, and surprised my sister Nancy, in a pleasant home. She had married a prosperous farmer, who owned the farm on which they lived, as well as some property in the city near-by. Mother was indescribably happy in finding her child so pleasantly situated, and took much pleasure with her bright little grandchildren; and after a long visit, returned home, although strongly urged to remain the rest of her life with Nancy; but old people are like old trees, uproot them, and transplant to other scenes, they droop and die, no matter how bright the sunshine, or how balmy the breezes.

On her return, mother found me with Mrs. Elsie Thomas, where I had lived during her absence, still sewing for a livelihood. Those were the days in which sewing machines were unknown, and no stitching or sewing of any description was allowed to pass muster, unless each stitch looked as if it were a part of the cloth. The art of fine sewing was lost when sewing machines were invented, and though doubtless they have given women more leisure, they have destroyed that extreme neatness in the craft, which obtained in the days of long ago.

Time passed happily on with us, with no event to ruffle life's peaceful stream, until 1845, when I met Frederick Turner, and in a few short months we were made man and wife. After our marriage, we removed to Quincy, Ill, but our happiness was of short duration, as my husband was killed in the explosion of the steamboat Edward Bates, on which he was employed. To my mind it seemed a singular coincidence that the boat which bore the name of the great and good man, who had given me the first joy of my meagre life—the precious boon of freedom—and that his namesake should be the means of weighting me with my first great sorrow; this thought seemed to reconcile me to my grief, for that name was ever sacred, and I could not speak it without reverence.

The number of killed and wounded were many, and they were distributed among friends and hospitals; my husband was carried to a friend's, where he breathed his last. Telegraphs were wanting in those times, so days passed before this wretched piece of news reached me, and there being no railroads, and many delays, I reached the home of my friend only to be told that my husband was dead and buried. Intense grief was mine, and my repining worried mother greatly; she never believed in fretting about anything that could not be helped. My only consolation from her was, "'Cast your burden on the Lord.' *My* husband is down South, and I don't know where he is; he may be dead; he may be alive; he may be happy and comfortable; he may be kicked, abused and half-starved. *Your* husband, honey, is in heaven; and mine—God only knows where he is!"

In those few words, I knew her burden was heavier than mine, for I had been taught that there was hope beyond the grave, but hope was left behind when sold "down souf"; and so I resolved to conceal my grief, and devote myself to my mother, who had done so much and suffered so much for me.

We then returned to St. Louis, and took up the old life, minus the contentment which had always buoyed us up in our daily trials, and with an added sorrow which cast a sadness over us. But Time, the great healer, taught us patience and resignation, and once more we were

> *"Waiting when fortune sheds brightly her smile,*
> *There always is something to wait for the while."*

VII

Four years afterward, I became the wife of Zachariah Delaney, of Cincinnati, with whom I have had a happy married life, continuing forty-two years. Four children were born to us, and many were the plans we mapped out for their future, but two of our little girls were called from us while still in their childhood. My remaining daughter attained the age of twenty-two years, and left life behind, while the brightest of prospects was hers, and my son, in the fullness of a promising youth, at the age of twenty-four, "turned his face to the wall." So my cup of bitterness was full to the brim and overflowing; yet one consolation was always mine! Our children were born free and died free! Their childhood and my maternity were never shadowed with a thought of separation. The grim reaper did not spare them, but they were as "treasures laid up in heaven." Such a separation one could accept from the hand of God, with humble submission, "for He calleth His own!"

Mother always made her home with me until the day of her death; she had lived to see the joyful time when her race was made free, their chains struck off, and their right to their own flesh and blood lawfully acknowledged. Her life, so full of sorrow, was ended, full of years and surrounded by many friends, both black and white, who recognized and appreciated her sufferings and sacrifices and rejoiced that her old age was spent in freedom and plenty. The azure vault of heaven bends over us all, and the gleaming moonlight brightens the marble tablet which marks her last resting place, "to fame and fortune unknown," but in the eyes of Him who judgeth us, hers was a heroism which outvied the most famous.

I FREQUENTLY THOUGHT OF FATHER, and wondered if he were alive or dead; and at the time of the great exodus of negroes from the South, a few years ago, a large number arrived in St. Louis, and were cared for by the colored people of that city. They were sheltered in churches, halls and private houses, until such time as they could pursue their journey. Methought, I will find him in this motley crowd, of all ages, from the crowing babe in its mother's arms, to the aged and decrepit, on whom the marks of slavery were still visible. I piled inquiry upon inquiry, until after long and persistent search, I learned that my father had always lived on the same plantation, fifteen miles from Vicksburg. I wrote to my father and begged him to come and see me and make his home with me; sent him the money, so he would be to no expense, and when he finally reached St. Louis, it was with great joy that I received him. Old, grizzled and gray, time had dealt hardly with him, and he looked very little like the dapper master's valet, whose dark beauty won my mother's heart.

Forty-five years of separation, hard work, rough times and heart longings, had perseveringly performed its work, and instead of a man bearing his years with upright vigor, he was made prematurely old by the accumulation of troubles. My sister Nancy came from Canada, and we had a most joyful reunion, and only the absence of our mother left a vacuum, which we deeply and sorrowfully felt. Father could not be persuaded to stay with us, when he found his wife dead; he longed to get back to his old associations of forty-five years standing, he felt like a stranger in a strange land, and taking pity on him, I urged him no more, but let him go, though with great reluctance.

THERE ARE ABOUNDING IN PUBLIC and private libraries of all sorts, lives of people which fill our minds with amazement, admiration, sympathy, and indeed with as many feelings as there are people, so I can scarcely expect that the reader of these episodes of my life will meet with more than a passing interest, but as such I will commend it to your thought for a brief hour. To be sure, I am deeply sensible that this story, as written, is not a very striking performance, but I have brought you with me face to face with but only a few of the painful facts engendered by slavery, and the rest can be drawn from history. Just have patience a little longer, and I have done.

I became a member of the Methodist Episcopal Church in 1855; was elected President of the first colored society, called the "Female Union," which was the first ever organized exclusively for women; was elected President of a society known as the "Daughters of Zion"; was matron of "Siloam Court," No. 2, three years in succession; was Most Ancient Matron of the "Grand Court of Missouri," of which only the wives of Masons are allowed to become members. I am at present, Past Grand Chief Preceptress of the "Daughters of the Tabernacle and Knights of Tabor," and also was Secretary, and am still a member, of Col. Shaw Woman's Relief Corps, No. 34, auxiliary to the Col. Shaw Post, 343, Grand Army of the Republic.

Considering the limited advantages offered me, I have made the best use of my time, and what few talents the Lord has bestowed on me I have not "hidden in a napkin," but used them for His glory and to benefit those for whom I live. And what better can we do than to live for others?

Except the deceitfulness of riches, nothing is so illusory as the supposition of interest we assume that our readers may feel in our affairs; but if this sketch is taken up for just a moment of your life, it may settle the problem in your mind, if not in others, "Can the negro race succeed, proportionately, as well as the whites, if given the same chance and an equal start?"

"The hours are growing shorter for the millions who are toiling;
And the homes are growing better for the millions yet to be;
And we all shall learn the lesson, how that waste and sin are spoiling
The fairest and the finest of a grand humanity.

It is coming! it is coming! and men's thoughts are growing deeper;
They are giving of their millions as they never gave before;
They are learning the new Gospel; man must be his brother's keeper,
And right, not might, shall triumph, and the selfish rule no more."

Finis

A Note About the Author

Lucy A. Delaney (1830–1891) was an African American author and activist. Born into slavery in St. Louis, Missouri, she was the daughter of Polly Berry, a freeborn woman from Illinois who had been stolen into slavery as a young girl. In 1843, after multiple escape attempts and years of waiting for her cases to be heard, Polly won two separate lawsuits in St. Louis to earn freedom for herself and her daughter. Two years later, Lucy married Frederick Turner and moved to Illinois with him and her mother, but was forced to return to Missouri shortly thereafter following Turner's death in a steamboat boiler explosion. In 1849, she married Zachariah Delaney, with whom she would have four children. Alongside her husband, Delaney was an active member of the African Methodist Episcopal Church and a supporter of local health and education initiatives. In addition, she served as president of both the Female Union, an organization for African American women, and the Daughters of Zion, an affiliate group of the Freemasons. At the age of 52, Delaney was reunited with her father 45 years after he was sold down the Mississippi River to a plantation owner in the deep south. In the last year of her life, Delaney published *From the Darkness Cometh the Light: Or, Struggles for Freedom* (1891), a memoir and slave narrative which remains the only known firsthand account of a freedom suit.

A Note from the Publisher

Spanning many genres, from non-fiction essays to literature classics to children's books and lyric poetry, Mint Edition books showcase the master works of our time in a modern new package. The text is freshly typeset, is clean and easy to read, and features a new note about the author in each volume. Many books also include exclusive new introductory material. Every book boasts a striking new cover, which makes it as appropriate for collecting as it is for gift giving. Mint Edition books are only printed when a reader orders them, so natural resources are not wasted. We're proud that our books are never manufactured in excess and exist only in the exact quantity they need to be read and enjoyed.

bookfinity™

Discover more of your favorite classics with Bookfinity™.

- Track your reading with custom book lists.
- Get great book recommendations for your personalized Reader Type.
- Add reviews for your favorite books.
- AND MUCH MORE!

Visit **bookfinity.com** and take the fun Reader Type quiz to get started.

Enjoy our classic and modern companion pairings!

Classic & Modern

www.ingramcontent.com/pod-product-compliance
Lightning Source LLC
Chambersburg PA
CBHW020447030426
42337CB00014B/1438